the**bush**theatre

The Bush Theatre presents the world premiere of

How To Curse

by Ian McHugh

10 October – 10 November 2007

Cast

Miranda	**Emily Beecham**
William	**Robert Boulter**
Nick	**Al Weaver**

Director	**Josie Rourke**
Designer	**Christopher Oram**
Lighting Designer	**Hartley TA Kemp**
Sound Designer	**Jack C Arnold**
Assistant Director	**Sam Yates**
Deputy Stage Manager	**Marie Costa**
Casting	**Chloe Emmerson**
Production Photographer	**Nobby Clark**

How To Curse received its world premiere performance at
The Bush Theatre, London, on 10 October 2007.

How To Curse was developed with the support of New River Dramatists, North
Carolina, and Old Vic New Voices, London.

Ian McHugh would like to thank everyone who has helped in the development
of this script, particularly Patricia McHugh, Ellie Rycroft, Beth Tilston,
Clarissa Ford, Jennie Syson, Sarah Glenny, Dasha Shenkman, Christopher
Oram, Sam Yates, Emily Beecham, Robert Boulter and Al Weaver. Special
thanks to Nathaniel J. Miller, Fay Davies and Josie Rourke.

Quotations from *The Waves* by Virginia Woolf by permission of the Society of
Authors, as the literary representative of the estate of Virginia Woolf.

Emily Beecham Miranda

Emily graduated from LAMDA in 2006.

TV includes: *Lewis: Series II* (ITV); *The Bill* (Talkback Thames); *New Tricks* (BBC); *Miss Marple: Bertram's Hotel* (ITV); *Party Animals* (BBC/World Productions); *The Innocence Project: Series I* (BBC/World Productions); *Bon Voyage* (ITV/Box TV); *Afterlife* (ITV).

Film includes: Emily has just finished filming a leading role in *The Calling* (Vermillion Films); *Rise of the Footsoldiers* (Carnaby Films/Optimum); *28 Weeks Later* (DNA Films/Searchlight); *The Calling* (MEDB Films) and *God's Wounds* (RSA Films).

Comedy: *Later at the Bush: The Callous Corruption of Wesley McBunyion.*

Robert Boulter William

Theatre includes: *Herons* (Royal Court); *Moonfleece* (National Theatre Workshop); *Karamazoo* (Theatre by the Lake, Keswick); *Mercury Fur* (Menier Chocolate Factory); *Burn/Chatroom/Citizenship* (National Theatre).

TV includes: *Judge John Deed* (BBC); *The Long Firm* (BBC); *Waking the Dead* (BBC).

Film includes: *Daylight Robbery* (Giant Films); *Donkey Punch* (WarpX Films).

Radio includes: *The Fall and Rise of Danny Clark* (BBC R4).

Al Weaver Nick

Theatre includes: *The Waltz of the Toreadors* (Chichester); *What Light Through Yonder Window Breaks* (Soho Theatre); *Coram Boy* (National Theatre); *Malvolio and his Masters* (Southwark Playhouse); *All the Ordinary Angels* (Manchester Royal Exchange); *Hamlet* (Old Vic Theatre); *Red Hot Promise* (National Theatre) and *Catalogue of Misunderstanding* (Young Vic Studio).

TV includes: *Five Days* (HBO/BBC); *Viva Blackpool* and *Inspector Lynley* (BBC); *Planespotting* (Granada).

Film includes: *Marie Antoinette* (Focus Features); *Doom* (Universal); *The Merchant of Venice* (Sony Pictures); *Colour Me Kubrick* (Magnolia Pictures); *The Story of...* (Short) and *Islands of the City* (Short).

Ian McHugh Writer

Ian McHugh was born in Norfolk. He studied at the Norwich School of Art and Design and gained an MA in Creative Writing from the University of East Anglia. He took part in Old Vic New Voices Departures project, writing four monologues in voices from Shakespeare for a promenade performance at the Old Vic, and has since supplied additional text for the 2005 RSC production of Massinger's *Believe What You Will*. *How To Curse* is his first original play.

Josie Rourke Director

Training: resident assistant director at the Donmar Warehouse to Michael Grandage, Nicholas Hytner, Phyllida Lloyd and Sam Mendes; assistant director to Peter Gill on *Luther* (NT) and *The York Realist* (ETT at the Royal Court and on tour); trainee Associate Director at the Royal Court Theatre.

Josie was the Associate Director of Sheffield Theatres and is the Artistic Director of The Bush. *How To Curse* is her first production at The Bush.

Other work as a director includes: *Loyal Women* and *Crazyblackmuthafuckin'-Self* (Royal Court); *The Cryptogram*, *World Music* and *Frame 312* (Donmar Warehouse); *Believe What You Will* and *King John* (RSC); *The Long and the Short and the Tall*, *Much Ado About Nothing*, *The Unthinkable*, *World Music* and *Kick for Touch* (Sheffield Theatres); *My Dad's A Birdman* (Young Vic); *Romeo and Juliet* (Liverpool Playhouse). Josie has directed the *24Hour Plays* at the Old Vic and on Broadway.

Christopher Oram Designer

Recent theatre work includes: *King Lear* and *The Seagull* (RSC); *Frost/Nixon* (Donmar/West End/Broadway); *Evita* (Adelphi); *Don Carlos* (Sheffield and West End); *Good*, *Passion Play*, *Privates on Parade*, *The Vortex*, *Henry IV*, *The Bullet*, *Don Juan in Soho*, *Grand Hotel*, *World Music*, *Merrily We Roll Along*, *Caligula* and *Parade* (Donmar Warehouse). Christopher has also designed costumes for the forthcoming film adaptation of *The Magic Flute*.

Hartley TA Kemp Lighting Designer

Theatre includes: *Gaslight* (Old Vic), *The Voysey Inheritance*, *Elmina's Kitchen*, *Scenes from the Big Picture* (National); *Romeo and Juliet*, *The Merry Wives of Windsor*, *Coriolanus* (RSC); *Kiss of the Spider Woman*, *Days of Wine and Roses*, *Passion Play*, *Good* (Donmar); *The York Realist* (English Touring Theatre/Royal Court); *Mrs Warren's Profession* (Strand); *Nakamitsu* (Gate, London); *American Buffalo* (Gate, Dublin); *Metamorphosis* (Lyric Hammersmith); *The Field* (Tricycle); *The Rubenstein Kiss* (Hampstead); *Certain Young Men*, *The Doctor's Dilemma* (Almeida); *The Birthday Party* (Birmingham Rep); *Arcadia*, *The Rivals*, *Loot*, *Paradise Lost*, *The Comedy of Errors*, *The Caretaker* (Bristol Old Vic); *A Number*, *Gladiator Games*, *A Midsummer Night's Dream*, *Original Sin*, *The Tempest*, *Don Juan*, *The Country Wife*, *As You Like It* (Sheffield); *Rutherford and Son* (Royal Exchange, Manchester).

Musicals include: *Miss Saigon* (Gothenburg Opera); *Showboat*, *West Side Story* (Tiroler Landestheater, Innsbruck); *Promises, Promises* (Sheffield Crucible); *The Wizard of Oz* (Birmingham Rep).

Opera includes: *Les Pêcheurs des Perles*, *Iris* (Holland Park); *Mary Seacole*, *Oreste*, *Oresteia* (English Bach Festival, ROH Linbury Studio); *M Butterfly*, *Martha*, *The Barber of Seville*, *La Sonnambula*, *Carmen* (Castleward Opera, Belfast).

Hartley is also Artistic Director of C venues at the Edinburgh Fringe.

Jack C Arnold Composer/Sound Designer

Film scores include: *The Open Doors* with Michael Sheen; *Oh Marbella!* with Rik Mayall and Mike Reid; *Cubs* for Free Range Films (Best British Short at 2006 BIFA, and nominated for a BAFTA); and most recently *The Beckoning Silence*, sequel to the acclaimed *Touching the Void*.

Theatre includes: Justin Butcher's plays *Breaking Strain* and *The Madness of George Dubya*; and Colin Teevan's *Missing Persons: Four Tragedies and Roy Keane* with Greg Hicks. He also designed sound and composed music for Simon Bent's hit adaptation of *Elling* starring John Simm, which transferred to the West End from The Bush Theatre.

TV includes: various dramas and documentaries, including *Timewatch*; and he will be scoring *The Last Van Helsing* for ITV in early 2008.

Sam Yates Assistant Director

Directing credits include: *The Turke* (Arcola); *Orpheus* and O*edipus, Son of Iocasta* (Poynton Theatre); *Odysseys and Oddities* (St Julian Warehouse Theatre, Lisbon); *Purgatory* by W.B. Yeats (C Venues, Edinburgh Fringe). Directing credits while at university include: *Macbeth* (Edinburgh Festival and ADC Cambridge); *The Tempest*, *Twelfth Night* and *Servants and Masters* (Homerton Auditorium, Cambridge).

As assistant director: *Hysteria* by Terry Johnson, directed by Paul Raffield; *Uncle Vanya*, directed by Rachel Kavanaugh (Birmingham Rep); *Wise Children* (workshop) adapted by Bryony Lavery, directed by Phyllida Lloyd (National Theatre Studio).

Sam has worked as a Broadcast Assistant to BBC Radio Drama on over twenty productions.

The Bush Theatre

'One of the most experienced prospectors of raw talent in Europe'
The Independent

The Bush Theatre is one of the most celebrated new-writing theatres in the world. We have an international reputation for discovering, nurturing and producing the best new theatre writers from the widest range of backgrounds, and for presenting their work to the highest possible standards. We look for exciting new voices that tell contemporary stories with wit, style and passion and we champion work that is both provocative and entertaining.

With around 40,000 people enjoying our productions each year, The Bush has produced hundreds of groundbreaking premieres since its inception 34 years ago. The theatre produces up to eight productions of new plays a year, many of them Bush commissions, and hosts guest productions by leading companies and artists from all over the world.

The Bush is widely acclaimed as the seedbed for the best new playwrights, many of whom have gone on to become established names in the entertainment industry, including Steve Thompson, Jack Thorne, Amelia Bullmore, Dennis Kelly, Chloë Moss, David Eldridge, Stephen Poliakoff, Snoo Wilson, Terry Johnson, Kevin Elyot, Doug Lucie, Dusty Hughes, Sharman Macdonald, Billy Roche, Catherine Johnson, Philip Ridley, Richard Cameron, Jonathan Harvey, Conor McPherson, Joe Penhall, Helen Blakeman, Mark O'Rowe and Charlotte Jones. We also champion the introduction of new talent to the industry, whilst continuing to attract major acting and directing talents, including Richard Wilson, Nadim Sawalha, Bob Hoskins, Alan Rickman, Antony Sher, Stephen Rea, Frances Barber, Lindsay Duncan, Brian Cox, Kate Beckinsale, Patricia Hodge, Simon Callow, Alison Steadman, Jim Broadbent, Tim Roth, Jane Horrocks, Mike Leigh, Mike Figgis, Mike Newell, Victoria Wood and Julie Walters.

The Bush has won over one hundred awards, and developed an enviable reputation for touring its acclaimed productions nationally and internationally. Recent tours and transfers include the West End production of *Elling* (2007), the West End transfer and national tour of *Whipping It Up* (2007), a national tour of *Mammals* (2006), an international tour of *After the End* (2005-6), *adrenalin... heart* representing the UK in the Tokyo International Arts Festival (2004), the West End transfer (2002) and national tour of *The Glee Club* (2004), a European tour of *Stitching* (2003), and Off-Broadway transfers of *Howie the Rookie* and *Resident Alien*. Film adaptations include *Beautiful Thing* and *Disco Pigs*.

The Bush Theatre provides a free script-reading service, receiving over 1000 scripts through the post every year, and reading them all. This is one small part of a comprehensive Writers' Development Programme, which includes workshops, one-to-one dramaturgy, rehearsed readings, research bursaries, masterclasses, residencies and commissions. We have also launched a pilot scheme for an ambitious new education, training and professional development programme, bushfutures, providing opportunities for different sectors of the community and professionals to access the expertise of Bush writers, directors, designers, technicians and actors, and to play an active role in influencing the future development of the theatre and its programme.

The Bush Theatre is extremely proud of its reputation for artistic excellence, its friendly atmosphere, and its undisputed role as a major force in shaping the future of British theatre.

Josie Rourke
Artistic Director

Fiona Clark
Executive Producer

At The Bush Theatre

Artistic Director	**Josie Rourke**
Executive Producer	**Fiona Clark**
General Manager	**Angela Bond**
Literary Manager	**Abigail Gonda**
Bushfutures Co-ordinator	**Anthea Williams**
Finance Manager	**Dave Smith**
Production Manager	**Robert Holmes**
Development Manager	**Sophie Hussey**
Development Officer	**Sara-Jane Westrop**
Chief Technician	**Tom White**
Resident Stage Manager	**Christabel Anderson**
Administrative Assistant	**Maxine Pemble**
Literary Assistant	**Jane Fallowfield**
Box Office Supervisor	**Ian Poole**
Box Office Assistants	**Charlotte Ive** **Catherine Nix-Collins**
Front of House Duty Managers	**Kellie Batchelor** **Adrian Christopher** **Abigail Lumb** **Glenn Mortimer** **Kirsten Smith** **Lois Tucker**
Duty Technicians	**Jason Kirk** **Esteban Nunez** **Mark Selsby** **Shelley Stace**
Associate Artists	**Tanya Burns** **Es Devlin** **Chloe Emmerson** **Richard Jordan** **Paul Miller**
Pearson Writer in Residence	**Jack Thorne**
Press Representative	**Ewan Thomson & Giles Cooper at Barkowski**
Marketing	**Ben Jefferies at Spark Arts Marketing**

The Bush Theatre
Shepherd's Bush Green
London W12 8QD

Box Office: 020 7610 4224
www.bushtheatre.co.uk

The Alternative Theatre Company Ltd. (The Bush Theatre)
is a Registered Charity number: 270080
Co. registration number 1221968

VAT no. 228 3168 73

supported by

h&f
hammersmith & fulham

Be there at the beginning

Our work identifying and nurturing writers is only made possible through the generous support of our Patrons and other donors. Thank you to all those who have supported us during the last year.

If you are interested in finding out how to be involved, please visit the 'Support Us' section of www.bushtheatre.co.uk, or call 020 7602 3703.

bushfutures

The Bush Theatre has launched an ambitious new education, training and development programme, bushfutures providing opportunities for different sectors of the community and professionals to access the expertise of Bush writers, directors, designers, technicians and actors, and play an active role in influencing the future development of the theatre and its programme.

What to look out for:

Company Mentoring
Advice and support for emerging companies seeking support and expertise from The Bush.

Future Playwrights
Writing courses with Bush writers and staff, culminating in scratch showcase performances.

Bush Activists
A theatre group for 16+ who will study various aspects of theatre with professional practitioners.

Future Directors
Opportunities for new directors to work with professional directors and engage with The Bush.

School Projects
This season The Bush is working with schools in the area and giving students access to new writing, new writers and professional directors. If you are a teacher or student get in touch to see how we can work with your school.

If you'd like to find out more about how to get involved, please email bushfutures@bushtheatre.co.uk

HOW TO CURSE

Ian McHugh

Characters

MIRANDA

NICK

WILLIAM

They are all seventeen years old.

Setting

Nick's bedsit on Great Yarmouth seafront. A mattress on the floor, a few blankets, a TV and a Sony PlayStation 2. A full-length mirror rests against the wall. There is a bookcase, piles of books and more books strewn across the floor. There are two doors, one to the outside world and another to a bathroom.

How To Curse *was developed with the support of New River Dramatists, North Carolina, and Old Vic New Voices, London.*

This text went to press before the end of rehearsals and may differ slightly from the play as performed.

Scene One

NICK *plays on his Sony PlayStation.* MIRANDA *reads Virginia Woolf's* The Waves.

MIRANDA. 'I have lost friends, some by death . . . others through sheer inability to cross the street.' Isn't that great?

NICK. 'I am not so gifted as at one time seemed likely. Certain things lie beyond my scope. I shall never understand the harder problems of philosophy.'

Beat.

MIRANDA. How do you do that?

NICK. Magic.

Scene Two

NICK *enters,* WILLIAM *follows.*

They pull chocolate bars from their pockets, then CDs and DVDs. They each take off their jackets followed by a series of shirts with price tags still attached.

NICK *reaches into a tear in the lining of his jacket and pulls out several paperback books.*

WILLIAM. Books? That's bollocks, mate. What did you get?

He picks up a few of the books.

Of Mice and Men . . . Brave New World . . . To the Lighthouse . . . There was a film about her. Had Liz Taylor in it.

NICK. Who?

WILLIAM. You at college then?

No response.

WILLIAM *unzips his jeans and pulls three satsumas from inside. He offers one to* NICK.

NICK. . . . No thanks.

WILLIAM. You should eat more fruit. You'd have better skin.

NICK. What's wrong with my skin?

NICK *takes a satsuma, peels and eats it.* WILLIAM *looks around the flat.*

WILLIAM. I've got a PlayStation. Well, my mate has.

Beat.

Nice place.

NICK. Yeah? I'm on a waiting list.

WILLIAM *makes himself at home on the mattress.*

WILLIAM. So where do you go out?

NICK. Go out?

WILLIAM. At night. What do you do?

NICK. I don't go out.

WILLIAM. What do you do?

NICK *shrugs.*

Beat.

I went to a great party last weekend. Up near Holkham. Took acid. Went skinny-dipping. Got an ear infection. You got any food?

NICK. No.

WILLIAM. Well, are you going to offer me anything to drink?

NICK. Would you like something to drink?

WILLIAM. Got any vodka?

NICK. Uh . . .

WILLIAM. Beer?

NICK. . . . No. Sorry.

WILLIAM. Cup of tea? Anything'll do.

NICK. I don't have any tea. Or cups.

WILLIAM. What do you use to drink?

NICK. The bottle. The tap.

WILLIAM. That's disgusting.

> NICK *goes into the bathroom.* WILLIAM *glances at himself in the mirror.*

You got a girlfriend?

> NICK *returns and hands* WILLIAM *a bottle of whisky.*

Nice one.

Beat.

Want to see my scar?

NICK. Scar? What scar?

WILLIAM. Appendix.

> *He lifts up his T-shirt and shows* NICK *a scar on his belly.*

You can touch it if you want.

NICK. Really?

WILLIAM. Course. Wouldn't have said so, would I?

> NICK *runs his finger over it.*

> WILLIAM *takes the bottle of whisky and drinks. He watches* NICK *intently as he studies the scar.* NICK *looks up and* WILLIAM *quickly looks away.*

> NICK *takes the bottle from* WILLIAM *and drinks.*

NICK. Well, here's my comfort.

WILLIAM. This is alright. Own bathroom. Sea view. You made it sound like a proper fucking hole in the ground. You're right round the corner from the arcades. And like a million take-aways. Be fucking great to live here.

NICK. Where do you live?

Beat.

WILLIAM. Not round here.

NICK. You live on your own?

Beat.

WILLIAM. With my mum.

NICK. Oh, right.

WILLIAM. Yeah. It's not good. Her bloke . . .

NICK. What about your dad?

WILLIAM. Dead. A long time ago. Buried at sea.

NICK. You're kidding.

WILLIAM. Got a photo. Want to see?

WILLIAM *pulls a photo from his wallet;* NICK *pores over it.*

NICK. He's very young.

WILLIAM. Yeah.

NICK. I like his uniform.

WILLIAM. Do you?

Pause.

NICK. I'm sorry.

WILLIAM. Well, it was a long time ago.

NICK. I saw a guy jump in front of a train.

WILLIAM. What?

NICK. It was slowing down but he jumped up. Caught him mid-air.

WILLIAM. Jesus Christ. That's fucked up.

NICK. It was beautiful. Like an explosion, or a star going super-nova. He just . . . leapt up.

WILLIAM. Jesus. That must've hurt like fuck.

NICK. It looked really quick.

WILLIAM. Why would someone do something like that?

NICK. Life is as tedious as a twice-told tale vexing the dull ear of a drowsy man.

WILLIAM. Huh?

NICK. . . . Nothing.

WILLIAM. My mum says life's about enduring pain. I don't know. We're Catholic so, you know . . .

Pause.

So. Is this . . . something you do often?

NICK. What's that?

WILLIAM. You know – this.

NICK. What?

WILLIAM. This kind of thing. You know, in Superdrug.

Beat.

Cruising the aisles . . .

Beat.

A casual glance over the Pantene . . .

NICK. Huh?

WILLIAM. I've heard about people like you.

NICK. You have?

WILLIAM. Conflicted young men in their late teens hanging round shopping malls on the lookout for like-minded individuals. Usually carrying a skateboard.

NICK. I don't . . . skate.

WILLIAM. No, that's not what –

NICK. I thought I recognised you.

WILLIAM. Really?

NICK *nods*.

I knew I'd seen you around, but . . .

He looks at NICK, *intrigued*.

Your face. It's familiar.

NICK. It is?

WILLIAM. Yeah. Really . . . familiar.

WILLIAM *purposefully sits back on the mattress*.

This where you sleep?

NICK. Uh, yeah.

WILLIAM. Comfortable.

NICK. It's okay.

WILLIAM. I love to . . . sleep. Sleep all the time if I could.

NICK. Last night I dreamt bees were making me into honey.

WILLIAM (*sitting back up*). What?

NICK. . . . Nothing. It's just . . . No, nothing.

WILLIAM. No, what?

NICK. It's just . . . You've never had that dream?

Beat.

Or the one where you're already honey, and people are like, spreading you on their toast.

WILLIAM. No, mate, I don't think I have.

NICK. There's another one, where I'm lying on my bed in my old room, and the pillow is full of bees. And then the mattress. And the sheets.

WILLIAM *recoils at the idea of this*.

No, they're nice bees. They're soft. They don't sting. They wouldn't sting you. It's just that they . . . All that air moving around under their wings. They tickle. And the whole room just sort of . . . thrums. And then . . .

Beat.

WILLIAM. S'okay, I mean, my dreams are like, totally fucked up. I dreamt I was Beyoncé.

NICK. Beyoncé?

WILLIAM. Yeah. It's not always Beyoncé. Sometimes it's J-Lo. And then sometimes it's Janet Leigh, or Tippi Hedren. Or Christina Aguilera.

NICK (*looking blank*). Aguilera?

WILLIAM. You know Kim Novak?

NICK (*lying*). Yeah.

WILLIAM. Sometimes her.

Beat.

Got any more of that?

NICK *passes the bottle.* WILLIAM *takes a very large gulp and falls deliberately onto the mattress.*

NICK. You okay?

WILLIAM. Yeah, I'm fucking flying.

NICK. You are?

WILLIAM. Most definitely.

NICK. Like you're in a squall.

WILLIAM. Huh? Yeah. One of those.

NICK. So you know what it's like.

WILLIAM. Hmm?

NICK. Being caught in a storm.

WILLIAM. Mmm. Suppose.

NICK. At sea?

WILLIAM. My dad told me never to go to sea.

NICK. No, that's wise.

WILLIAM. Never go to sea and never marry a woman who eats chips in bed.

NICK *(his reverie broken)*. . . . What?

WILLIAM sits up and looks at him, smiles.

They look at each other for a long moment.

Want to play a game?

WILLIAM. A game?

He looks to the PlayStation.

What you got?

NICK sits opposite WILLIAM on the mattress.

NICK. Close your eyes.

WILLIAM smiles and closes his eyes. NICK follows suit.

Now you have no idea how far this room stretches on. It could go on for ever.

WILLIAM opens his eyes.

It dilates. Black hems at the outer reaches. Can you feel the boat rocking?

WILLIAM. You've lost me, mate.

NICK opens his eyes.

NICK. Close your eyes.

WILLIAM closes his eyes.

Feel it now?

WILLIAM. Er . . .

NICK. Are you a conjurer?

WILLIAM *(coyly)*. Well . . . I might be.

NICK. We'll contrive a shipwreck.

He lights a match and lifts WILLIAM's forearm.

He rolls up the sleeve, blows out the match, and presses it quickly to WILLIAM's skin.

WILLIAM *flinches and pulls his arm away sharply.*

WILLIAM. Jesus Christ!

He punches NICK *in the shoulder, hard.*

What did you do that for? You fucking –

He punches NICK *again.*

NICK. Don't –

WILLIAM. What's wrong with you?

He gets up and starts to pull on his jacket.

NICK. No, don't . . .

WILLIAM. Fuck sake.

NICK. Please. I didn't mean to.

WILLIAM. Fuck you.

He ties his shoelaces in a hurry.

NICK. No, wait.

WILLIAM. What's your problem?

NICK. Please. Don't. I didn't mean to.

Pause.

You can sleep over.

WILLIAM *hesitates, then takes off his jacket.*

Scene Three

NICK *is silently crying.* MIRANDA *enters.*

NICK. And where the fuck were you?

MIRANDA. What?

NICK. I waited half a fucking hour.

MIRANDA. I didn't see you.

NICK. I was where you fucking left me.

MIRANDA. Why didn't you just get yourself a drink?

NICK (*mimicking her*). 'Why didn't you just get yourself a drink?'

MIRANDA. A little shandy to calm you down perhaps?

NICK. Wanker wouldn't serve me.

MIRANDA. That's not my problem.

NICK. Well, whose is it then?

MIRANDA. I'm not your fucking mother.

NICK. I fucking hate that pub.

MIRANDA. I rather like it.

NICK. You're an embarrassment.

MIRANDA. He bought me a drink. What, you want me to just take his drink and walk away?

NICK. He was all over you.

MIRANDA. So? I like him.

NICK. Everyone was staring at you.

MIRANDA. Fuck were they. You were staring at me.

NICK. I was not.

MIRANDA. Better watch yourself. Staring at girls like a fucking psycho.

Beat.

NICK. Give me your key.

Beat.

She realises her error.

I want your key back.

MIRANDA. Oh, come on.

NICK. Give me back my key. You've lost my trust.

MIRANDA. I'm just fucking around. I didn't mean –

NICK. Yeah, whatever.

He backs off.

Pause.

MIRANDA. You alright?

He shrugs.

You didn't have to just shoot off like that.

Pause.

I'll rub your shoulders.

Beat.

NICK. Okay.

She rubs his shoulders.

Pause.

MIRANDA. I liked that book.

NICK. Yeah? She drowned.

MIRANDA. You're kidding. That's horrible. The poor woman . . .

NICK. She did it on purpose.

MIRANDA. Oh. Well, in that case.

NICK. I've got some more if you want?

He finds Virginia Woolf's Orlando *from a pile of books on the floor and hands it to* MIRANDA.

It's about a man who turns into a woman.

MIRANDA. Great. Spoil the ending for me why don't you.

Pause.

So who was that bloke at the bar?

NICK. What bloke?

MIRANDA. The one you were staring at, before you were staring at me.

NICK. I wasn't staring at you, I don't know what you're talking about.

MIRANDA. Yes you do. Who was he?

NICK. I don't know. Just someone.

Beat.

MIRANDA. Is this the bloke you've been on about?

NICK. I don't know.

MIRANDA. You don't know?

NICK. It might be him.

MIRANDA. Either it is or it isn't.

NICK. I think it's him.

MIRANDA. You think?

NICK. Okay, yes, it's him.

MIRANDA. You're sure? Point him out to me. I'll have a word.

NICK. A word?

MIRANDA. I'll talk to him, I'll say I'm a friend of yours and –

NICK. No. He won't know me. He won't remember me. No, don't.

She sits back and sighs.

Don't be like that.

MIRANDA. Like what?

NICK. It won't work without him.

MIRANDA. If it works at all.

NICK. It won't work without him.

MIRANDA. Yeah. Right.

NICK *sighs angrily.*

You can't just ask a random stranger to –

NICK. He's not a stranger.

MIRANDA. Whatever, you let this bloke in, he might not think it's . . .

NICK. What?

MIRANDA. He might not have your sense of humour.

NICK. This isn't funny.

She smirks.

Oh fuck off.

MIRANDA. Fuck off yourself.

NICK (*mimicking*). 'Fuck off yourself.' Stupid bitch.

She hits him hard.

MIRANDA. What's your fucking problem?

Pause.

He picks up a book from the floor.

NICK. Have you read this one?

MIRANDA. I'm not fucking reading Hemingway.

NICK. Why not? Fuck you then. What about *The Bell Jar*?

MIRANDA. I read that like five times when I was fourteen.

NICK. Keats?

MIRANDA. A thing of beauty is a joy forever –

NICK (*quickly, derisively*). Its loveliness increases, it will never pass into nothingness, but will still keep a bower quiet for us, and a sleep full of sweet dreams.

MIRANDA. Keats sucks arse.

NICK. Baudelaire?

MIRANDA. It's in translation. You have to read it in the French.

NICK. I don't know 'the' French. Read some fucking Judy Blume then.

MIRANDA (*knowing he has*). Have you got any?

Beat.

NICK. No.

MIRANDA. Are you there, God? It's me, Miranda. I'm stuck in a filthy fucking hovel at the arse end of the world with a fucking retard who smells of piss and shit and cum and has a reading age of five.

He stares her out, unimpressed.

She takes a breath, changes tack.

Come on. It's still early. Where do you want to go? The beach?

He grunts a reluctant 'yes', pulls some clothes from the floor and goes into the bathroom.

If you're lucky I'll buy you some candyfloss and doughnuts.

He returns wearing different jeans.

NICK. I'd rather have a toffee apple.

He lifts a T-shirt from the floor and sniffs it.

MIRANDA. I wasn't kidding, you reek.

NICK. Fuck off.

MIRANDA. Seriously, let me buy you some fucking shower gel.

NICK. It's not like your personal hygiene's beyond reproach. Could smell you before you came in the door.

MIRANDA. If I close my eyes and wish very, very hard, is it possible you might go and fuck yourself?

NICK. You must be rotting or something. Thou deboshed fish thou!

She slaps him.

MIRANDA. We should wash your mouth out with soap and water.

NICK. I wish you would.

She looks at him squarely for a long moment. He kisses her on the lips; she remains impassive.

I do begin to have bloody thoughts.

She laughs, then gets up and goes into the bathroom.

He looks at himself in the mirror.

Scene Four

Morning. WILLIAM *wakes up on the floor.*

He sees NICK *asleep on the mattress and realises where he is. He's wide awake in an instant.*

He quickly slips on his socks but then can't find his shoes. He quietly searches the room but to no avail.

He looks at NICK *for a long moment.*

He looks around the room again, his patience wearing thin.

WILLIAM (*quietly*). Oi.

No response.

Oi, Nick.

Pause.

NICK *stirs a little.*

Nick, where are my shoes, mate?

NICK *is suddenly still again.*

Nick.

Beat.

Nick. Come on, wake up. What have you done with my shoes?

NICK *stirs again, grumpily.*

Come on, I need my shoes.

NICK *gives him a cursory glance then heads into the bathroom.*

Where are my fucking shoes?!

The sound of a toilet flush. NICK *returns.*

17

NICK. Want to play *Tomb Raider*?

Beat.

No? *Vice City*?

WILLIAM. Where are my shoes?

NICK *ignores him.*

Come on, give them back. For fuck sake.

Pause.

Fine. I'll walk home in my socks. Send my fucking mate round to fucking sort you out. He bought me those shoes.

He goes to the door. It's locked. He rattles it. He kicks it.

Jesus fucking Christ!

He turns back to NICK.

Unlock the door.

NICK. Sit down.

WILLIAM. Unlock it.

NICK. Sit down.

WILLIAM. Unlock it or I'll scream.

NICK. You won't scream.

Pause.

WILLIAM *is suddenly very scared.*

WILLIAM. I have to go.

NICK. No you don't.

WILLIAM. This isn't funny.

NICK. No, I know.

Beat.

I know who you are.

WILLIAM. Who am I then?

NICK. I recognised you.

18

A long pause.

NICK *puts a game into the PlayStation.*

You want to watch or you want to play too?

WILLIAM *stares at* NICK. NICK *smiles back.*

Come on . . .

No response.

He turns back to the game: a car revs, screeches to a halt, gunfire; the car screeches, crashes. Game over.

Fuck sake.

He throws down the controller.

WILLIAM (*terrified*). I have to go. Now.

NICK. No. I need your help.

WILLIAM. Now. I need to go now. Please. I won't tell anyone I was here.

NICK. Just . . . wait.

WILLIAM. Please. Please. My arm hurts. Look at my arm.

He rolls up his sleeve.

You did that.

NICK. I'm sorry. I already said I was sorry.

WILLIAM. That's . . . that's fucking assault.

NICK *looks at him blankly.*

He looks back, and starts to build an idea of NICK's *intentions.*

Pause.

NICK. I want to try again.

WILLIAM. Try what again?

NICK. Close your eyes.

WILLIAM. No. Look . . . No, okay? Let's get this clear. I'm not closing my eyes and I'm not letting you tie me up, or –

NICK. Why would I tie you up?

WILLIAM. I don't know. You look the type.

NICK. I'm not going to tie you up.

WILLIAM. No, I fucking know you're not.

Beat.

NICK. Please, just –

WILLIAM. I'm not closing my eyes! Who the fuck are you? I
don't know . . .

NICK. Please. I want to try again.

WILLIAM. Yeah?

NICK. I'm asking nicely.

WILLIAM. This is nicely?

Pause.

Something in WILLIAM *– a thread of self-preservation – gives
way. He begins taking off his clothes.* NICK *looks on, stunned.*

NICK. What are you doing?

WILLIAM. If I want to stop, we stop. Okay? I have to trust you.

NICK. You can trust me.

WILLIAM. Yeah, well, I have to know that for myself. You know?

NICK. Okay. Whatever.

WILLIAM. It's not that I don't want to. But . . .

NICK. You can trust me.

WILLIAM. Can I?

NICK. Yeah.

Beat.

WILLIAM. Okay.

Beat.

WILLIAM *is now in his underwear.* NICK *is very disconcerted.*

20

In addition to the scar on WILLIAM*'s belly there are conspic-
uous scars on his upper body.*

Okay?

Beat.

NICK. Yeah.

Beat.

WILLIAM. Well, come on then.

Beat.

NICK. Right. Yeah.

Beat.

Now. Close your eyes.

WILLIAM *closes his eyes.*

Okay. Can you feel the boat rocking?

WILLIAM (*opening his eyes*). Do you have to do all that shit?
Can't we just –

NICK. Close your eyes.

Beat.

WILLIAM *closes his eyes again.*

We're going to contrive a shipwreck.

WILLIAM (*opening his eyes*). What? No. What does that mean?
A shipwreck?

NICK. Close your eyes.

WILLIAM *keeps his eyes wide open.*

NICK *hesitates.*

He moves closer to WILLIAM, *and looks him in the eye. He's
scared though he holds the gaze as long as he can.*

WILLIAM *looks back, bewildered.*

NICK *turns* WILLIAM *around in his arms and examines his
shoulder blades. He studies him closely, as a doctor would.*

He sniffs him.

He rests his ear against WILLIAM*'s back, and after a moment reaches a hand around and presses it to* WILLIAM*'s chest.*

Pause.

WILLIAM. What are you doing?

He moves around and sits in front of WILLIAM *once more. He looks again into* WILLIAM*'s eyes, though this time with an anxious disappointment.* WILLIAM *is ever more bewildered.*

He presses his hands against WILLIAM*'s ears and closes his eyes. He concentrates and his breath becomes strained.*

Then suddenly he stops.

NICK. I thought you were the one.

Pause.

WILLIAM. And am I?

Pause.

NICK. Are you sure you don't remember?

WILLIAM. Remember what?

NICK. You flamed amazement.

WILLIAM. I did what?

NICK. You divided and burned, flamed distinctly. Jove's lightning, thunder; with fire and cracks you invoked Neptune. His waves rose and trembled. Men jumped overboard with their hair on fire, screaming, 'Hell is empty and all the devils are here.'

Beat.

No?

WILLIAM *shakes his head.*

Are you sure?

WILLIAM. Can you hear yourself?

NICK. What do you mean?

Beat.

Don't fucking take the piss.

WILLIAM. I'm not. It's just –

NICK. I can see it.

He looks down at the floor.

And I can see you. Lifting up the edges of the sea and flicking it like a rug. I can see it like it's now. I can hear it.

He looks back up at WILLIAM, *expectantly.*

You . . .

WILLIAM. . . . . Yes . . . ?

NICK. It's you . . .

WILLIAM*'s phone rings. He pulls it from his pocket, looks at the number. He puts it back in his pocket and waits for it to stop ringing.*

Silence.

WILLIAM. Please. Please can I have my shoes back?

Pause.

I have to go sometime.

NICK. Why?

WILLIAM. I just do.

NICK *lies down on the mattress.* WILLIAM *looks around the room.*

Have you, like, read all these books?

Scene Five

A song plays on the stereo. MIRANDA *puts on large headphones and plugs them in. She turns the volume way up and breaks the seal on a bottle of whisky.*

She closes her eyes and dances, bottle in hand. She sings along under her breath.

NICK *enters carrying books. He pulls the headphones cord from the stereo; music blasts out of the speakers.* MIRANDA *opens her eyes and takes off the headphones.*

He adjusts the volume then snatches the whisky from her and takes a big gulp. He spits it straight back out.

MIRANDA. Don't waste it.

NICK. It's foul.

MIRANDA. Drink up. Go on, it'll do you good.

He takes a sip, grimaces.

Now swallow.

He does.

Better?

NICK. Mmm. Ow . . .

He clutches his stomach.

MIRANDA (*taking the bottle*). Have you eaten today?

NICK. Give me that.

He snatches the bottle, takes a bigger gulp, grits his teeth and swallows.

(*With a wry smile.*) You'll never guess what I found.

MIRANDA. No, probably not. What have you found?

NICK. I had to leave it outside.

NICK (*turning down the volume*). William.

MIRANDA. That's what I said.

NICK. Don't start.

MIRANDA. I'm not starting. Don't you fucking start.

NICK. And that's all you got?

MIRANDA. What more do you want? His phone number?

NICK *snatches the bottle, drinks.*

He told me he's going shopping for a new pair of jeans tomorrow.

NICK. So?

MIRANDA. I told him he'd look good in a pair of Diesel.

NICK. And?

MIRANDA. How many places sell Diesel in this town? I was thinking I might go shopping too, and just coincidentally run into him.

NICK. No.

MIRANDA. No? I thought you might like to come along. You could do with some new clothes.

Beat.

NICK. I can do it on my own.

MIRANDA. He doesn't know you. He hasn't met you. You need me there.

NICK. I can't talk to him with you breathing down my neck.

MIRANDA. I don't think he'll be best pleased when some freaky unwashed boy starts following him round town reciting *Hamlet* at him.

NICK. This has fuck all to do with *Hamlet*. Leave him out of this.

MIRANDA. Well, whatever crap you spout to turn a gentleman's head.

NICK. . . . *What?*

MIRANDA. You can't hang around the precinct all day on your own. Security'll clock you and you'll get barred and they'll put that picture of you on the noticeboard again.

NICK. I'll be subtle.

MIRANDA. Yeah, right.

NICK. I can be subtle.

MIRANDA. Yeah, and I can be fucking Kate Moss.

Beat.

Look. You want this to work, don't you?

He sighs.

Come here.

He goes to her. She cradles him.

You haven't changed your mind, have you?

NICK. No, course not. But –

MIRANDA. But what?

He shrugs in mild despair.

Pause.

The heavens will open.

He's not convinced.

The sky will light up.

NICK. Yeah?

MIRANDA. Well, that's what you told me.

NICK. Yeah. Yeah, it will.

Beat.

Breathe in.

She does.

Beat.

Can you feel it?

She nods.

He holds her and slowly rocks her back and forth.

The ship were no stronger than a nutshell.

MIRANDA. And as leaky as an unmanned wench.

NICK. Unstanched.

MIRANDA. What?

NICK. As leaky as an unstanched wench.

MIRANDA. What does that mean?

NICK. Er . . .

MIRANDA. And then the ship splits in two, doesn't it?

NICK. It does.

Beat.

MIRANDA. It'll be beautiful.

Pause.

Meet me outside Burger King at one.

Scene Six

NICK *and* WILLIAM, *as before.*

NICK. I want to go home.

WILLIAM. You are home. I want to go fucking home.

NICK. I want to go home.

WILLIAM. Yeah? Where's home then?

Beat.

NICK. I want to go –

WILLIAM. Yeah, but where?

NICK. We could go to the beach.

WILLIAM. You lived on the beach?

NICK gives him a disparaging look.

I went to Ibiza last summer. Ended up sleeping on the beach. Got bitten to fuck.

Pause.

NICK. You know what you can help me with?

WILLIAM. What?

NICK. A murder.

Beat.

WILLIAM. A murder. Who do you want to murder?

NICK. I don't know. Someone. A man.

WILLIAM. I don't think that's a good idea.

NICK. No, you're right. Once a man indulges himself in murder, very soon he comes to think little of robbing; and from robbing he comes next to drinking and Sabbath-breaking, and from that to incivility and procrastination.

Pause.

I don't want to kill anyone. I just want to set fire to everything they have. Then watch them kill themselves.

WILLIAM. It proper turns you on, huh?

NICK. What?

WILLIAM. All that stuff. Death, destruction and shit. I've met blokes like you before but they usually wear black nail varnish and have like, piercings, everywhere.

NICK. You what?

WILLIAM. What's so fucking great about death?

NICK (*deadly serious*). It's quiet.

WILLIAM. No shit.

NICK. And there's no time.

WILLIAM. It's fucking forever!

NICK. Time can only exist when it has an end.

WILLIAM *laughs*.

Do you ever think about the moment of your death?

WILLIAM. You what?

NICK. Can you picture it? Can you see yourself there?

WILLIAM. Why would I want to?

NICK. You must know it's coming. Like when you sense someone coming up behind you. Or when you know someone else
is in the room. And then it's in you. And then it *is* you.

WILLIAM *laughs in disbelief*.

What's funny?

WILLIAM. You. Making a tent in your trousers with all this shit.

NICK. Making a tent?

WILLIAM. No wonder your sheets are like a board. Blistered
palms, I don't doubt.

NICK. You saying I masturbate too much?

WILLIAM (*taken aback*). Well, yeah, I suppose that's what I was
getting at but –

NICK. How much is too much?

WILLIAM. It was a joke.

Beat.

Just want to watch you don't do yourself an injury.

NICK. An injury? What kind of injury?

WILLIAM. Well, I don't know – it's a minefield really. Might
dislocate your wrist or something. Take your eye out . . .

NICK (*panicked*). My eye?

WILLIAM. Christ, don't have a heart attack. Forget what I just
said; do it as often as you like.

NICK. Do you call it 'masturbating'?

WILLIAM. Only when I'm talking to a priest.

Beat.

We could have a wank now if you like.

Beat.

NICK. What do you mean?

WILLIAM. If you want to.

NICK. If I want to?

WILLIAM. Don't you?

NICK. What do you mean? Now?

WILLIAM. Why not?

NICK. Here?

WILLIAM. . . . Yeah.

Beat.

NICK. No.

WILLIAM. Fine. It was just an idea.

NICK. No.

WILLIAM. Okay.

Beat.

I'm hungry.

NICK. In the bathroom. There's some biscuits in the cabinet.

WILLIAM *gets up quickly and goes into the bathroom. NICK goes to the bookshelf. He pulls a knife from inside a copy of* Heart of Darkness.

WILLIAM *returns, a pack of digestives in his hand, two or three biscuits in his mouth.*

WILLIAM (*talking with his mouth full*). You want one?

NICK. No, you're alright.

WILLIAM. These are really good. Any drink left?

NICK hands him the bottle. WILLIAM drinks.

NICK. We should try again.

WILLIAM. I don't think so. Whatever we're trying to do, it isn't
working. Why don't you play your game again. Or something
else. What else you got?

NICK. No, I want to try again.

Pause.

WILLIAM. Look, this isn't working out like you'd planned, is it?
And it really isn't working out like I thought it would. So how
about we cut our losses, eh?

NICK picks up the knife.

What's that for?

NICK stares at WILLIAM, speechless.

Is that for you or for me? 'Cause I've got no problem sticking
it in you. Ever since you stuck a match in my arm.

Beat.

He quickly snatches the knife from NICK's hand.

NICK is angry and panicked. WILLIAM looks him in the eye.

You're into some weird shit. I mean, what's *this*?

No response.

I know people like you.

NICK. You do?

WILLIAM. So what are you into?

NICK. What am I into?

WILLIAM. Yeah. Tell me.

NICK. Tell you what?

WILLIAM. You just need to . . . let go, right?

Beat.

You can hit me, if you want.

NICK *backs off*.

Go on. Hit me.

Beat.

Come on, mate, I don't let just anyone hit me.

NICK. I don't want to hit you.

WILLIAM. I'm inviting you to.

Pause.

NICK *hits him in the chest, not very hard*.

No, come on, harder than that.

NICK. I've never hit anyone before.

WILLIAM. Seriously? I don't believe you.

WILLIAM *lifts the knife and holds it across his chest*.

You need to let go a bit, mate.

NICK. What are you –

He adds pressure to the knife then quickly pulls it away. A fine line of blood appears.

Fuck! What are you doing? Don't!

WILLIAM. It's not deep.

He runs a finger along the wound, collecting the blood. He licks it.

It's surface. Just a scratch. You want a go?

NICK. No!

WILLIAM. On me.

He takes off his shirt.

Go on.

He tries to give the knife to NICK. NICK *refuses to take it. He pulls a small knife from his pocket*.

Take it.

NICK *does*.

It's very sharp. Much sharper than your stupid bread knife. So be gentle. Go on. Anywhere. I'll close my eyes. I won't look. Go on.

He closes his eyes. Holding the knife, NICK *touches* WILLIAM's *chest.*

Take your time . . .

NICK *looks at himself in the mirror, and takes off his own shirt. He holds the knife, runs it over his own chest and down to his stomach.*

He pushes it in, drawing blood. He runs a finger through it, lifts it to his mouth.

WILLIAM *opens his eyes.*

What the . . . Jesus! What are you doing?

NICK. I . . .

WILLIAM. You twat, you've got it everywhere.

NICK. I'm sorry.

WILLIAM. Christ. It's not difficult to follow simple instructions.

NICK. I just –

WILLIAM. Come here. You're a fucking mess.

NICK. I'm sorry.

WILLIAM. It's okay. Just . . . hold this.

He gives NICK *his shirt to stop the blood.*

Now hold it tight. Oh fuck. We should go to A and E.

NICK. There's no need.

WILLIAM. It's deep. You're not supposed to do it like that, you fucking moron.

NICK. It's not that deep.

WILLIAM. Yeah, it is.

NICK pulls the shirt away, looks at the wound.

NICK. You're right. Feels like the flesh is peeling off me.

WILLIAM. Hold it tighter!

He looks around the room for a better bandage.

Fuck . . .

NICK. Now you'll have to stay.

Scene Seven

MIRANDA, *alone*.

As she speaks she performs a magic trick: she passes a green handkerchief through her closed fist several times; on the final pass it becomes a red handkerchief.

MIRANDA. Haven't you ever really wanted it? On one of those nights when the flies are buzzing round your face and sticking to your skin, and the back of your neck itches and you can hardly breathe? Haven't you ever just wanted to see the sky light up and have the wind blow you sideways and the thunder press against your throat?

And what comes after. The stillness. The debris. How things have shifted and realigned. New configurations. Imbalances righted.

He had me half-convinced. I egged him on. Of course, I didn't know how to do it, and nor did he. But it has to be possible, right?

She laughs.

No, me neither. But there was something beautiful about the way he worked. He wouldn't give up. Someone must know.

It's convincing, isn't it? All these books. All those words, strung together. It's like a spell. It is a spell. It's very clever, how convincing it is. It's a whole world; it exists, real as any other world. And it grabs hold of you, it drags you in. To the point at which your own world ceases to exist.

(As she completes the trick.) Come unto these yellow sands.

Scene Eight

Darkness. WILLIAM*'s forgotten mobile phone lights up and rings.*

The sound of footsteps approaching outside.

The phone stops ringing. NICK *and* WILLIAM *enter the room.* NICK *flicks on the light. He sits down and takes off his shoes.*

WILLIAM. Jesus, your feet stink.

NICK *rubs at his wound and winces.* WILLIAM *shoots him a look. His phone rings again.*

WILLIAM *picks it up and looks at the number. He answers, moves away from* NICK *to talk.*

What?

So?

I don't care.

I'm staying at a friend's.

No one you know.

What's it got to do with you anyway?

I don't need your money.

It's none of your fucking business.

No.

Oh, go fuck yourself.

He hangs up.

NICK *sniffs at his shirt.*

You want to have a bath or something?

NICK. Can't get the stitches wet.

WILLIAM. I'm not giving you a bed-bath.

Beat.

Does it hurt?

NICK. What?

WILLIAM. The stitches.

NICK. Only when I bend.

WILLIAM. Then don't bend.

Pause.

It is okay, if I . . . you know?

NICK. What?

WILLIAM. Stay over.

NICK. Yeah. Do what you want.

WILLIAM. But you want me to, right?

NICK. Want you to what?

WILLIAM. Stay.

NICK. Yeah, whatever.

WILLIAM. Okay. Well, in that case, I'll head off.

NICK. What?

WILLIAM. I'll get going. You're alright now, right? You're sorted?

NICK. I'm fine.

WILLIAM. Course. You're fit as a fiddle.

Beat.

Well, see you then.

He goes to the door. NICK *tries to stand, winces.* WILLIAM *turns and gives him a look.*

NICK. I'm fine.

WILLIAM. Right. Bye then.

NICK. Bye.

He winces. WILLIAM *stops in his tracks.*

Pause.

You'll have to sleep on the floor again.

WILLIAM. We could top and tail.

Pause.

WILLIAM *sits down next to* NICK. NICK *takes hold of* WILLIAM's *forearm.*

He studies it, weighs it in his hand, as if surveying a fish he's caught. He's mesmerised.

He looks up at WILLIAM, *mouth open.* WILLIAM *is equally perplexed.*

You want to take a bath? With me?

NICK. Can't get the stitches wet.

WILLIAM. I'll be careful.

NICK *stares at the floor.*

Scene Nine

WILLIAM *is asleep on the mattress.* MIRANDA *stands in the doorway watching, livid.*

She enters the room quietly, and makes herself at home. She plays with a cigarette lighter – flicking it to make it spark, occasionally letting it flame.

She pulls her copy of The Waves *from her bag, opens the book and begins to read aloud, purposefully.*

MIRANDA. 'The sun had not yet risen. The sea was indistinguishable from the sky, except that the sea was slightly creased

41

as if a cloth had wrinkles in it. Gradually as the sky whitened a dark line lay on the horizon dividing the sea from the sky and the grey cloth became barred with thick strokes moving, one after another, beneath the surface, following each other, pursuing each other, perpetually.'

WILLIAM. What are you doing here?

MIRANDA. Where's Nick?

WILLIAM sits up sharply and looks around.

Don't worry. I'm sure he's fine.

WILLIAM. No.

MIRANDA. No?

WILLIAM. Uh . . . He . . .

MIRANDA. What?

WILLIAM (*still sleepy*). No. He . . . What are you doing here?

MIRANDA. Where's Nick?

Beat.

WILLIAM. He had an accident.

MIRANDA. What kind of accident?

Beat.

WILLIAM. With a . . . (*Tries to mime 'knife'; fails.*) He cut himself.

She's distressed, then angry, then resigned.

MIRANDA. But he's okay?

WILLIAM. More or less. It wasn't serious.

MIRANDA. How serious?

WILLIAM. What do you mean?

MIRANDA. Did you go to the hospital?

WILLIAM. Uh, yeah. He had stitches.

MIRANDA. And they didn't want to keep him in?

WILLIAM. No. I don't know. I'm sorry. It was an accident.

MIRANDA. I doubt it. He was showing off. Take everything he says with a pinch of salt. I'm sure he's spun you an immaculate web of lies. Especially about me.

WILLIAM. He hasn't mentioned you.

MIRANDA. Really?

Beat.

WILLIAM. Look, I should go.

MIRANDA. No, stay. He'll be back soon. He'd kill me if he found out you were here and I let you go.

WILLIAM. He'd kill you?

MIRANDA. Well, he'd be really fucked off.

WILLIAM. Yeah, I bet.

He starts to get out of bed.

MIRANDA. Are you good at maths?

WILLIAM. What?

MIRANDA. Are you good at maths?

WILLIAM. Why?

MIRANDA. I'm a psychic mathematician.

WILLIAM. You're what?

MIRANDA. Think of a number between one and ten. Humour me. Come on, think of a number.

Beat.

WILLIAM. What is this?

MIRANDA. Just do it. Come on.

WILLIAM. I've just woken up!

MIRANDA. Think of a number. Don't tell me what it is. Multiply it by nine. You have a two digit number?

WILLIAM. . . . . Yeah.

MIRANDA. Add the two digits together.

WILLIAM. Okay.

MIRANDA. Are you there?

WILLIAM. I'm there.

MIRANDA. Now subtract five.

WILLIAM. Okay.

MIRANDA. Right. Now think of the letter of the alphabet that corresponds to that number. Like one is A, two is B, three is C, and so on.

WILLIAM. Okay.

MIRANDA. Now think of a country that begins with that letter.

WILLIAM. Okay.

MIRANDA. And think of an animal that begins with the second letter of that country.

WILLIAM. Okay, I'm there.

MIRANDA. Denmark. Elephant.

Beat.

WILLIAM. How . . . ?

MIRANDA. Magic.

WILLIAM *nods in amazement.*

Pause.

She holds up her book.

You want to hear some more of this?

WILLIAM. No thanks, that's okay.

MIRANDA. It's really good. You know what happened to her?

WILLIAM. No, what?

MIRANDA. Do you read?

WILLIAM. Yes, I can read. I'm not a retard.

MIRANDA. No. *Do* you read?

WILLIAM. Yeah. Of course I read.

MIRANDA. Who?

WILLIAM. What?

MIRANDA. Which writers?

WILLIAM. Uh, I don't know. Lots of different writers.

MIRANDA. Have you read Proust?

WILLIAM. No.

MIRANDA. You should – he's awesome. And F. Scott Fitzgerald.
And Louis de Bernières.

Beat.

WILLIAM. Look, I'll –

MIRANDA. No –

He hesitates.

Let me read your palm. Go on. I have the gift. It's uncanny.
Give me your hand.

He does.

So soft! What do you use?

WILLIAM. Nothing . . .

MIRANDA. Lack of hard work.

WILLIAM. Ha. That's what you think.

MIRANDA. Water hands. Unusual for a man.

WILLIAM. What does that mean?

MIRANDA. You're always in tune with your feelings, conscious
and unconscious. And you're intuitive, bordering on psychic.

WILLIAM. Is that right?

MIRANDA. Yeah. And it means you can be a great friend.

He snorts.

Let me guess. You're a Cancer, a Scorpio or a . . . Pisces.

WILLIAM. Virgo.

MIRANDA. Water is the element of the poet. You're always ready and willing to plunge yourself into a world of fantasy.

WILLIAM. I think you've got the wrong bloke.

MIRANDA. Troubled past.

He snorts again.

But a bright future. A new love on the horizon.

WILLIAM. Yeah?

MIRANDA. Yeah.

WILLIAM. I don't think you're very good at this.

MIRANDA. No, really, I see a change for you. Someone with dark hair.

WILLIAM. You can tell that from my hand.

MIRANDA. You'd be surprised.

WILLIAM. I fucking would.

MIRANDA. Oh!

WILLIAM. What?

MIRANDA. Your lifeline, it's –

WILLIAM. What?

MIRANDA. Do you have a history of illness in your family?

WILLIAM. Not that I know of.

MIRANDA. I just don't see . . . I don't see you as an old man.

WILLIAM. Oh.

MIRANDA. Lots of children though.

WILLIAM. Really? How many?

MIRANDA. Uh . . . Two.

He laughs.

I'm still learning.

WILLIAM. Yeah?

He stands up, and pulls on his jeans. He looks around the room for his jacket.

She reaches for her bag.

MIRANDA. Got some Stellas in here. You want one?

Beat.

WILLIAM. Go on then.

She pulls four cans of Stella from her bag, breaks off a couple, and hands one to him.

They drink.

WILLIAM *picks up some sunglasses from the floor.*

These yours?

MIRANDA. Nick's. You like them?

WILLIAM. They look expensive.

MIRANDA. He didn't buy them. Have them. He never wears them.

WILLIAM. No, I –

MIRANDA. Have them. Seriously.

WILLIAM. . . . Thanks.

He tries them on, looks in the mirror.

MIRANDA. They suit you.

He takes them off, embarrassed.

WILLIAM. So what do you do? You and Nick, when you –

MIRANDA. Did he tell you I was his girlfriend?

WILLIAM. No. I –

MIRANDA. We don't do anything. Seriously – nothing. Just hang round town and take the piss out of people. It's tragic.

Beat.

He'll want to see you.

WILLIAM. Yeah, but –

MIRANDA. And you'll want to see him. And then, seeing as we all know each other now, we can all go down the pub.

WILLIAM. Yeah, but –

MIRANDA. So you live round here?

WILLIAM. Yeah. No, I –

MIRANDA. You do or you don't?

WILLIAM. Yeah, I do.

MIRANDA. Whereabouts?

WILLIAM. Off Regent Road.

MIRANDA. On your own?

He tries to remember what he told NICK.

WILLIAM. Uh, no, with my –

MIRANDA. I've got to get a place of my own.

WILLIAM. Yeah?

MIRANDA. My dad's a total cock. Talks to me like I'm ten. I'm not ten; I have a driving licence for fuck sake.

WILLIAM. Do you?

MIRANDA. He's so fucking arrogant. And he lies. All the time. The things that come out of his mouth. Just bullshit. I mean – fuck – his whole job, what he does, is just a big fucking con.

WILLIAM. What does he do?

MIRANDA. He's a magician.

Beat.

WILLIAM. A magician. Like bunnies out of hats?

MIRANDA. He doesn't use animals. He's not allowed to any more.

WILLIAM. Does he saw people in half?

MIRANDA. Yeah. He used to practise on me.

WILLIAM. That's so fucking cool. How does he do it? What's the secret?

MIRANDA. I can't tell you that.

WILLIAM. No?

MIRANDA. No. Want to see my scar?

WILLIAM. Huh?

MIRANDA. I'm kidding.

WILLIAM. I have a scar. Want to see?

MIRANDA. Not particularly.

WILLIAM. I don't mind.

MIRANDA. I'm sure you don't.

He lifts his T-shirt and shows her the scar on his belly.

WILLIAM. Appendix.

MIRANDA. Appendix is on the other side.

He pulls down his T-shirt, embarrassed.

WILLIAM. So . . . what other tricks does your dad do?

MIRANDA. I don't know – all of them.

WILLIAM. Does he do the ball under the cups one?

MIRANDA. Yeah. That's kids' stuff.

WILLIAM. The one where you tear up the five-pound note and then you get it back in one piece?

MIRANDA. Yeah, but you have to do it with a twenty at least, or else no one gives a fuck.

WILLIAM. Does he do the guillotine thing?

MIRANDA. Yeah.

WILLIAM. Levitation?

MIRANDA. Yeah, that's another one I used to help with.

WILLIAM. He'd make you levitate?

She nods.

I saw a girl levitate once.

MIRANDA. You did not.

WILLIAM. I did. Laura O'Neill. Sat next to me in French.

MIRANDA. Bullshit.

WILLIAM. It's true. In PE. She fell off the wall-bars. Except she didn't hit the floor. She nearly did but she stopped a couple of centimetres above, just for a second. Weird stuff always used to happen to Laura.

MIRANDA. Like Sissy Spacek in that film.

WILLIAM. I love that film.

MIRANDA. Yeah, it's amazing.

WILLIAM. The bit in the shower!

She stares at him blankly.

When they all throw the . . .

MIRANDA. What?

WILLIAM. You know, the other girls, when they all . . .

MIRANDA. What?

WILLIAM. No, nothing. You've seen the film, right?

MIRANDA. Course.

WILLIAM. When she . . . You know, in the shower. And she doesn't know what's happened to her. And she's like . . .

He does a passable impression of Sissy Spacek in the opening scene of Carrie.

MIRANDA *slowly shakes her head.*

No?

Beat.

It doesn't matter.

MIRANDA. No, go on, tell me. I didn't see that bit.

WILLIAM. It's right at the beginning.

MIRANDA (*suddenly*). You think he's a virgin?

WILLIAM. Who?

MIRANDA. Nick.

WILLIAM. I don't know. Probably. I don't know.

MIRANDA. Are you?

WILLIAM. God no.

MIRANDA. No, you don't look like one.

WILLIAM. Uh, thanks.

MIRANDA. So, how did you two meet?

WILLIAM. Me and Nick?

MIRANDA. Yes, you and Nick.

WILLIAM. Uh . . . in town. He was buying shower gel.

MIRANDA. And you?

WILLIAM. Oh, I was just browsing.

MIRANDA. Browsing shower gel?

He shrugs.

He's cute, isn't he?

WILLIAM. He's alright.

MIRANDA. I met this bloke. Francis. You've probably seen him down the pub.

WILLIAM. No, I don't think so.

MIRANDA. Short hair, stocky, Adidas top.

WILLIAM. . . . Yeah, maybe . . .

MIRANDA. Always on the *Millionaire* machine.

WILLIAM. Bloke with the lisp!

MIRANDA. He doesn't have a lisp.

WILLIAM. Yeah, baseball cap and –

MIRANDA. He doesn't have a lisp.

WILLIAM. No? Can't be the same bloke then.

MIRANDA. He's a got a Stüssy cap and a –

WILLIAM. Key chain.

Beat.

She simmers.

Must be a different bloke.

MIRANDA. Did Nick tell you about the time he went to Italy?

Beat.

No? Last year. He booked a flight to Milan. He was planning to get a boat from there to . . . somewhere or other. Someone told him Milan was a port.

He hitched to some little town on the coast. Slept on the beach till he got hypothermia and the police picked him up and took him to hospital.

WILLIAM. He didn't tell me that.

MIRANDA. No? Did he tell you they won't have him in the house? His mum reckons he tried to kill his dad. They think he's the devil.

Beat.

No?

WILLIAM. You're making this up.

MIRANDA. God's honest truth. He was one of Mum's clients. Well, him and his mum and dad. You should see their file!

Beat.

I didn't tell you that. But really.

Beat.

WILLIAM. What?

MIRANDA (*shaking her head*). Nothing.

Beat.

No. I've said too much.

WILLIAM. You got any food?

MIRANDA. Though there was this time he came round the house. Followed her home.

WILLIAM. Who?

MIRANDA. My mum. Dad was livid. Got a bit aggro. It all got so fucked up. She nearly lost her job.

WILLIAM. There's some biscuits, somewhere, if you want one.

MIRANDA. What?

WILLIAM. Got any crisps?

Beat.

MIRANDA. What?

WILLIAM (*sighs*). Doesn't matter.

MIRANDA. Want to play a game?

WILLIAM (*nervous*). A game?

MIRANDA. Your choice. *Final Fantasy? Vice City?*

WILLIAM. I love *Vice City*.

MIRANDA. Have it. He never plays it.

WILLIAM. He was playing it yesterday.

MIRANDA. Have it.

NICK *comes in carrying supermarket bags and eating dough-nuts. The sight of* WILLIAM *and* MIRANDA *stops him in his tracks.*

MIRANDA *looks up and catches his eye.*

He burps.

O Captain! My Captain!

WILLIAM (*all smiles*). Alright?

MIRANDA *glares at* NICK, *unforgiving.*

NICK. What?

He glances at WILLIAM, *who is now looking through a pile of PlayStation games. He looks back to* MIRANDA, *who continues to stare at him with absolute surety.*

WILLIAM *is oblivious to this stand-off.*

WILLIAM. Have you got *Guitar Hero*?

NICK. What?

WILLIAM. We were going to play a game.

NICK. With her?

WILLIAM *nods.*

No. She's shit at everything.

MIRANDA *laughs.*

MIRANDA. I was just telling Will – do you mind if I call you Will? – I was just telling Will about last summer.

NICK. What about last summer?

MIRANDA. You know, the fun we had, the day trips –

NICK. I barely know her.

MIRANDA. . . . Those sultry afternoons –

NICK. Really, you don't want to listen to anything she says.

MIRANDA. . . . The time you set fire to your dad's car.

NICK. You weren't even there when that happened.

She smiles smugly.

MIRANDA. No, I wasn't. I didn't even know him then.

NICK. Leave me alone.

MIRANDA. But we had a lovely summer together. Took the Audi up into the hills, had picnics, drank wine. I prefer a dry Riesling; my companion, with his inferior palate, a Merlot.

WILLIAM. An Audi?

NICK (*to* MIRANDA). You can go now.

MIRANDA. He was such a sweet boy when I met him. Always on his best behaviour, the thieving and fire-starting aside. Impeccable table manners. The kind of boy you could trust with your nana. Not that I'd trust my nana with him.

NICK. I like your nana.

MIRANDA. See what I mean?

NICK. She looks like Dorothy Parker.

MIRANDA. Yeah. Didn't she have a go at herself with a blade?

She eyeballs NICK. *He puts a hand defensively to his stomach.*

Stitches?

He nods.

And they just let you go?

Beat.

What name did you give?

NICK. Tom Eliot.

She considers this.

MIRANDA. Yeah, that's better. Last time he said he was Alfred Lord Tennyson.

WILLIAM. Last time?

MIRANDA. Septicaemia. Dead badger.

NICK. They knew I wasn't Tennyson.

MIRANDA. You think?

WILLIAM. What were you doing with a badger?

MIRANDA. A creature of the isle!

WILLIAM. A what?

MIRANDA. For the storm. It was part of the . . . exercise.

WILLIAM. The exercise?

NICK. The badger was never going to work.

MIRANDA. No, and it stank. But we don't need it now.

NICK. No.

MIRANDA. We're all sorted now, aren't we?

WILLIAM (*laughs*). You're both mental.

MIRANDA. So the rumour goes. (*To* NICK.) So come on. Are you ready?

NICK. No. I told you –

MIRANDA. Oh, come on. We've been waiting for ages. Will wants to see what you're made of.

NICK. What I'm made of?

MIRANDA. Seriously, you wouldn't believe some of the shit we've tried. Fucking badgers, for fuck sake.

NICK. Miranda –

MIRANDA. And how many spells call for you to piss in a Starbucks cup and take a sip?

NICK. Shut up.

MIRANDA. Or paste pictures of Laurence Olivier all around the room. Or Kirk Douglas in a loincloth.

NICK. Shut up!

MIRANDA. Oh, was that not part of the spell? No?

NICK *glares at her.*

Pause.

She looks directly at NICK *and speaks with thinly veiled malice.*

How a ship having passed the line was driven by storms –

NICK. Don't.

MIRANDA. Yeah. This is part of the spell. And . . . Water, water, everywhere, and all the boards did shrink.

NICK. What the fuck do you think you're playing at?

MIRANDA. This bit's good. And some in dreams assured were, of the spirit that plagued us so. Nine fathom deep had he followed us, from the land of mist and snow.

WILLIAM. Yeah, I like that.

MIRANDA. It's good, isn't it?

She shoots NICK *a cold smile.*

And every tongue, through utter drought, was withered at the root; we could not speak, no more than if we had been choked with soot.

She looks to WILLIAM.

WILLIAM. Me?

MIRANDA. It's your line.

WILLIAM. My line?

She nods.

What do I say?

MIRANDA. What does he say, Nick?

NICK *stares at her.*

How does it go? The rest of the spell, how does it –

NICK. Stop it!

MIRANDA (*thinks hard*). Ah! Well a-day! What evil looks had I from old and young! Instead of the cross, the Albatross about my neck was hung.

NICK. Stop it! You're fucking it up!

She shoots him a wicked smile. She gets up and starts to assemble the items from earlier – the plastic windmills, sticks of rock, postcards, Frisbees, water pistols, snorkels, inflatable armbands, and gonks.

Don't. Please don't.

She ignores him.

Not now. We're not ready.

She finds two carrier bags of pebbles and empties them on to the floor.

She goes into the bathroom.

Please. Don't let her –

She returns dragging a large piece of driftwood – a staff.

WILLIAM. Jesus, where'd you find that?

She lets the staff drop to the floor.

MIRANDA. In the dunes. Took us an hour to get it back here. Driver wouldn't let us on the bus, would he?

NICK *stares at her, livid. She smiles back at him.*

NICK. You won't get away with this.

MIRANDA. With what?

NICK. I'll curse you.

MIRANDA. Like to see you try.

NICK. I'll turn you into a fucking crayfish.

MIRANDA (*laughs*). That's weak. I'll curse you, fucking have you ground into dust. Ground into dust and cut with cheap poxy speed and sold to kids under the pier who'll get washed out to sea and drown.

NICK. Fucking drown me? I'll have octopuses crawl inside you and –

WILLIAM. Octopi.

NICK. Octopuses!

MIRANDA. Octopodes, actually.

NICK. I'll have fucking octopuses lay their fucking eggs in you and have their little octo-babies burst out of your stomach and –

MIRANDA (*to* WILLIAM). Isn't that *Alien*?

WILLIAM. Yeah. Sigourney Weaver. That guy, John something.

NICK. No no no no –

MIRANDA. Yes it is.

NICK. Fuck you is it.

MIRANDA. It is. Now don't be a cunt about it.

NICK. Don't call me a cunt.

MIRANDA. Then don't be a cunt.

NICK. Don't call me a cunt.

WILLIAM. You want me to leave you two alone?

MIRANDA. How about I call you a pin-dicked river of sputum?

NICK. Fuck-witted cock-docker.

MIRANDA. Casting aspersions on my wit will get you nowhere.

NICK. You're supposed to be helping here.

MIRANDA. Darling, I wouldn't cum in your face if your eyes
    were on fire.

    WILLIAM *becomes ever more tense as the exchange
    continues.*

NICK. Why, thank you.

MIRANDA. You're welcome.

NICK. And I wouldn't break the seal on that putrid little box no
    other man will touch.

MIRANDA. No, too busy breaking into yourself with that fuck-
    ing PlayStation gamepad.

NICK. You fucking –

MIRANDA. Can't play *Tiger Woods PGA Tour* from in there.

NICK. Frigid whore.

MIRANDA. Ruptured arsehole.

NICK. Hag-born freckled whelp.

MIRANDA. Filthy misshapen knave.

NICK. Bitch.

MIRANDA. Cunt.

WILLIAM. Okay.

Beat.

MIRANDA. Okay what?

WILLIAM. How does this . . . work?

Beat.

This . . . spell? How does it? How do we . . . ?

MIRANDA *and* NICK *look at each other.*

What do we have to do?

MIRANDA. We . . .

She looks to NICK.

NICK. No.

WILLIAM. Why not?

NICK *looks to* MIRANDA.

Everything's ready. Right?

WILLIAM *gestures to the objects* MIRANDA *has assembled.*

MIRANDA. Yeah.

WILLIAM (*to* NICK). So why not? We're ready. Right? It's ready.

Beat.

NICK *can't quite believe it.*

NICK (*unsure*). Yeah. (*Then suddenly with certainty.*) Yeah.

He looks to MIRANDA.

A heavy pause.

Where from?

MIRANDA. Where from?

NICK. You are three men of sin?

MIRANDA. ... whom destiny, that hath to instrument this lower world and what is in it, the never-surfeited sea –

NICK. I have made you mad. I and my fellows are ministers of fate. The elements of whom your swords are tempered may as well wound the loud winds, or with bemocked-at stabs kill the still-closing waters, as diminish one dowle that's in my plume. My fellow-ministers are like invulnerable. The powers, delaying, not forgetting, have incensed the seas and shores, yea, all the creatures, against your peace.

Beat.

NICK's eyes are closed and his body is tense.

Silence.

WILLIAM. What's he doing?

MIRANDA hushes him.

NICK breathes heavily; he's oblivious to everything in the room. He mouths words, reciting a spell. He frowns and twitches. He appears to be in genuine torment. WILLIAM looks on.

MIRANDA turns her glance to WILLIAM, watches him watching.

He becomes more intense with every passing moment. Then ...

Nothing.

He's suddenly silent and still. He opens his eyes.

He looks around the room.

He looks at MIRANDA, then at WILLIAM.

Pause.

He is absolutely bereft.

NICK. It doesn't work.

MIRANDA. It doesn't?

NICK. No.

MIRANDA. How come?

NICK is in shock.

Well, that's a real pisser. Shall we go down the pub?

She breaks from the circle and goes into the bathroom.

NICK (*to himself*). It doesn't work.

WILLIAM. I almost thought it would.

NICK. It doesn't . . .

Beat.

WILLIAM. No.

Beat.

We could try again.

NICK. No.

Beat.

(*Suddenly ashamed.*) No.

MIRANDA *returns.*

MIRANDA. Are we ready? The pub?

NICK is oblivious.

Will?

WILLIAM. I don't know.

MIRANDA. Drinks are on me.

WILLIAM (*glancing at NICK*). Maybe in a bit.

MIRANDA. I don't want to come back and find you cut up in a bin bag.

WILLIAM. I think I'll stay.

Beat.

MIRANDA. Suit yourself.

She leaves.

Long pause.

WILLIAM *gets up and fetches the whisky. He takes a quick hit then offers it to* NICK. NICK *declines.*

Pause.

WILLIAM. You weren't here.

NICK. What?

WILLIAM. I was worried.

NICK. Why?

WILLIAM. What's in the bag?

NICK. Shopping. Plates, glasses . . . forks. Knives.

WILLIAM. Great. So when's the dinner party?

No response.

I'll help you knock up some spag bol. It's the only thing I know how to do. Except SuperNoodles.

NICK. I'm sorry. It was stupid.

Beat.

I thought . . .

Pause.

WILLIAM. Yeah, I get it.

NICK. It is in here. I just need to get it out.

WILLIAM. Yeah?

NICK. Yeah. It is.

WILLIAM. You should see a doctor.

NICK. I have seen a doctor.

WILLIAM. Yeah. So the doctor wasn't much help?

NICK. No. They just send me to sleep. Like I'm going to forget there.

WILLIAM. I know what you mean. When I was little, I thought there was a monster under my bed.

NICK. And was there?

WILLIAM. No, of course not.

NICK. You don't get it.

Beat.

WILLIAM. No. Sorry.

NICK. Can you see it? When you look at me, can you see it?

WILLIAM. I don't know what –

NICK. I took pictures of myself with my phone. I took my clothes off and took pictures in the mirror.

WILLIAM (*knowing*). Ha. Yeah . . .

NICK. But I couldn't see anything. So I tried with my dad's old camera. With the lights on, and then with the lights off. To see if there was a difference. To see if I'd . . . to see if there was a light. Or something. I thought I'd see something. I thought I'd see it in my bones. Or my head. Or here. (*Indicates his chest.*) Or here. (*Indicates his solar plexus.*)

WILLIAM. And did you?

NICK. They wouldn't give me the pictures. When I went to pick them up. I had to speak to the police. And a woman from Social Services.

Beat.

They spoke to my mum and dad. And . . .

Long pause.

WILLIAM. Let's take a look at those knives.

He picks a knife out of NICK's carrier bag, removes it from its packaging and runs the blade across his fingertips.

NICK. . . . Careful.

Pause.

WILLIAM. If you want . . .

He holds the knife out for NICK *to take.*

NICK. If I want . . .

WILLIAM. Please.

NICK. Uh . . .

NICK *takes the knife.* WILLIAM *unbuttons his shirt. He indicates a spot above his belly.*

WILLIAM. Here.

NICK. There.

WILLIAM. Yeah. Gently.

Long pause.

What's the matter?

NICK. I don't know.

WILLIAM. Don't you want to?

NICK. I don't know.

WILLIAM. Please.

NICK. I don't know.

WILLIAM *takes* NICK*'s hand and places it on the indicated spot. He holds it in position for a long moment then he lets his own hand drop.*

He kisses NICK *on the lips. He takes off* NICK*'s shirt, kisses* NICK*'s chest and stomach, and undoes his flies.*

What are you doing?

He starts to go down on NICK*. A few moments pass;* NICK *lifts* WILLIAM*'s head.*

No, no, stop, wait. Wait.

WILLIAM. What's the matter?

NICK. I want you to . . . Will you . . . will you put it in me?

WILLIAM. What?

NICK. You know. Your . . . sex.

WILLIAM. My what?

NICK. Your . . .

He gestures to WILLIAM's *crotch.* WILLIAM *tries not to laugh, but fails.*

WILLIAM. What?! Who . . . Where did you . . . Who calls it a 'sex'?

NICK. I don't know.

WILLIAM. Where did you . . . ?

NICK. I don't know. I thought that's what lovers called it.

WILLIAM. Lovers?

NICK. So will you?

WILLIAM *fumbles in his jacket pockets.*

WILLIAM. Hang on.

NICK. What for?

WILLIAM. I think I've got a . . . and some . . .

NICK *looks around the room. He catches his reflection in the mirror and holds its glance.*

WILLIAM *pulls a condom and some lube from a pocket.*

Here we go.

He begins pulling at NICK's *jeans.* NICK *resists.*

NICK. What's that?

WILLIAM. What's what?

NICK. That.

He picks up WILLIAM's *lube.*

WILLIAM. It's . . . well, it's –

NICK. You carry this around with you?

WILLIAM. Well . . . yeah.

NICK. You've done this before.

WILLIAM. Of course I've done this before.

Beat.

Can I stay here again? Tonight?

Beat.

Can I stay in your bed?

Beat.

Please.

WILLIAM *leans in and kisses* NICK. NICK *is unresponsive.*

What's the matter?

NICK *giggles.*

What?

NICK *looks at* WILLIAM *and laughs.*

What? What did I do?

Beat.

You want me to suck you off a bit more first?

NICK *stops laughing and pulls back further.*

WILLIAM. Or you want to give me a go?

NICK. You what?

WILLIAM. Come on.

WILLIAM *unzips his flies and tries to grab* NICK's *hand.*

Give me your hand.

NICK. Don't touch me.

WILLIAM *takes off his jeans.*

What are you doing? Get dressed.

WILLIAM. Come here.

NICK. She's waiting for us.

WILLIAM. So? Come here.

NICK *quickly pulls up his jeans and buttons his shirt.*

NICK. Get dressed.

WILLIAM (*desperately*). No, come here.

WILLIAM *reaches again to* NICK. NICK *flinches.*

Beat.

NICK. Touch me again, I'll cut off your hand.

WILLIAM *stands back in shock.*

Beat.

NICK *leaves.*

Silence.

WILLIAM *shakes.*

He stares violently into space.

Long pause.

He trains his eyes on a bookcase.

The books fly into the air and across the room.

He lies down on the mattress, dissipated.

Scene Ten

Sometime after midnight. MIRANDA *enters.*

She surveys the mess.

WILLIAM *enters from the bathroom, shirtless and drunk, the bottle of whisky in his hand.*

She sees his scars for the first time. She tries not to stare but can't help herself.

WILLIAM. I thought you were him.

68

MIRANDA. No such luck. Had a little fit, did he?

WILLIAM. Huh?

MIRANDA. He's like a fucking dervish when you set him off. He'll expect me to clean this up, you know.

WILLIAM. Have you seen him?

Beat.

MIRANDA. What are you still doing here?

He shrugs.

She looks around the room again.

I knew this would happen.

WILLIAM. Did you?

She sits back on the mattress and pulls a book from her bag. He catches her glancing at him.

She starts to read. He watches her.

Pause.

He stretches. She can't help but look.

MIRANDA. You should go.

WILLIAM. Have you noticed how he does that thing with his mouth right before he's about to say something? His lips . . .

Beat.

No?

Beat.

MIRANDA *is livid.*

MIRANDA. Do you ever get the urge to do purely wicked things, just for the sake of it?

WILLIAM. You don't know the half of it.

MIRANDA. Fuckwit.

WILLIAM. . . . Twat.

MIRANDA (*initiating a game*). Flat-footed dung-puncher.

WILLIAM. . . . Slut.

MIRANDA. Biscuit-faced freeloading cunt.

WILLIAM. Stupid . . . woman.

Beat.

She shakes her head in pity.

MIRANDA. You're wasting your time.

WILLIAM. He'll be back.

MIRANDA. Oh yeah? Where's he gone?

No response.

Have you scared him away?

Beat.

Would you like some help looking for your shoes?

WILLIAM. No, they're right here.

MIRANDA. Would you like some help tying your laces?

WILLIAM. What's your problem? (*Ire rising.*) He'd kill you if he knew I was here and you let me go.

MIRANDA. No, I think he's all done with you now.

Beat.

Won't someone be wondering where you are?

WILLIAM. I doubt it.

MIRANDA. Really?

WILLIAM. Really.

MIRANDA. I bet there's someone sitting at home –

WILLIAM. No –

MIRANDA. Listening out for the door –

WILLIAM. You don't know anything –

MIRANDA. Wondering where you –

The stereo turns itself on: radio static. It quickly tunes itself to the Shipping Forecast.

She's disconcerted; she quickly turns it off.

Pause.

Someone will be missing you.

WILLIAM. Do you see any search parties? I'm practically invisible.

MIRANDA. I can see you.

WILLIAM. Yeah, but you've got special powers, don't you? You and him, you see things that aren't there.

MIRANDA. It's a rare talent.

WILLIAM. It's fucking bullshit. It's a headcase and his hanger-on. A stuck-up little girl and her pet.

The insult hits home. She lets it sink in.

MIRANDA. Where is it you live?

WILLIAM. It's none of your fucking business, love.

MIRANDA. 'Cause I heard you stay with that guy who runs the comic shop. What's his name . . . ? Tony? Steve? No, wait. It's Mick, isn't it? Mickey with the funny eye.

WILLIAM. And what would you know?

MIRANDA. He's into the 'damaged' look then, is he?

He fronts her out.

The state of you. What kind of sick shit is that?

WILLIAM (*his patience breaking*). Oh, give it a fucking rest.

MIRANDA. Doesn't he mind?

WILLIAM. Fuck off.

MIRANDA. Or is this his handiwork? Is that it?

WILLIAM. Just –

MIRANDA. Does he get off on open wounds?

WILLIAM. Shut up.

The lightbulb fizzes.

MIRANDA. And what do you get out of it? You sick, dirty fucker.

A book flies from the bookcase and hits her.

WILLIAM (*with palpable fury*). Shut your mouth.

The lightbulb blows.

Pause.

I'm sorry. It's just . . . I didn't mean to . . .

MIRANDA *is dumbstruck. She looks at* WILLIAM *in disbelief.*

Beat.

He looks up at the light.

Shit. Got any spares?

Pause.

Could swap the one in the bathroom.

MIRANDA. What?

WILLIAM. I said, you could swap the one in the bathroom.

MIRANDA. No.

WILLIAM. No? Why not?

MIRANDA (*still in shock*). It won't come undone – the light in the bathroom.

WILLIAM. Could have a go.

He goes into the bathroom.

MIRANDA *stares after him.*

(*Off.*) Might need a chair to stand on.

Pause.

She tries to regain her composure.

MIRANDA. Listen, you couldn't go out and get a new one, could you?

WILLIAM *returns*.

WILLIAM. Now?

MIRANDA. There's an all-night offy at the end of the road – they might have one.

WILLIAM. Why do I have to go?

MIRANDA. You don't. If you don't want to.

Beat.

Are you hungry? There's a pizza place opposite. Open till one. You could just make it.

WILLIAM. Don't have any money.

She pulls a twenty-pound note from her purse.

Really?

She passes him the money, taking hold of his hand as she does. She holds it lightly for a moment, mesmerised.

Nivea.

MIRANDA. What?

WILLIAM. I lied. Hand cream. My mum says you can't start too young.

Beat.

You want one too? A pizza?

MIRANDA. No. I mean, yeah, okay.

WILLIAM. What kind?

MIRANDA. Whatever you're having.

Beat.

WILLIAM. Nice one.

He starts to go.

MIRANDA. What was it you called me?

WILLIAM. What? Oh no, ignore me. I'm a little cunt when you wind me up. Gets me into trouble.

MIRANDA. But what did you say? A stuck-up little girl?

WILLIAM. Jesus. Did I? Better watch my mouth.

MIRANDA. You better had.

He goes.

Pause.

She walks over to the stereo. She lifts her hand to turn it on. It turns on before she makes contact: The National Anthem plays. The music comes to a close and the radio turns itself off.

She picks up a book and looks at its cover. She looks at all the other books strewn across the room. She sits down among the books.

She continues to sit in silence for a long time.

NICK *enters, in a wretched state.*

NICK. Where is he?

He goes into the bathroom, re-emerges immediately.

Where is he? I need to see him.

No response.

I need to talk to him.

MIRANDA. He's not here.

NICK. Where is he then?

MIRANDA. . . . Just . . .

NICK. Did you see him?

No response.

What did he say?

Still nothing.

Oh fuck. Fuck.

Beat.

Fuck.

Pause.

Did he . . . ?

Beat.

Did he say . . . ?

Beat.

Did he say anything about –

MIRANDA. He didn't say anything about anything. Sit down.

NICK. Shut up. Don't tell me to sit down.

MIRANDA. Nick –

He notices the scattered books.

NICK. What have you done to my books?

MIRANDA. Nick . . .

NICK. What have you done? You fucking witch.

MIRANDA. Oh, is that what I am.

He looks at her with utter contempt.

NICK. You know, you should really just fuck off.

Beat.

She looks at him, angry, heartbroken. And ultimately resigned.

Really. Fuck off.

She laughs.

What?

MIRANDA. The things I do for you.

NICK. What the fuck have you ever done for me?

Pause.

MIRANDA. You were right about him.

NICK. Go away.

MIRANDA. He's the one you're looking for.

Beat.

You know he is.

Beat.

NICK. Don't take the piss.

MIRANDA. I'm not.

NICK. You are. It's a fucking sport to you.

MIRANDA. Nick –

NICK. No, don't even start with that. I know. Okay? I don't want to even think about that. Please. Let's just forget about it. Like it never –

MIRANDA. Listen –

NICK. I hate you. You think this is fucking hilarious, don't you? All that shit before. Making me do that. In front of him. Making me look like a fucking window-licker. I am such a twat. Oh, Jesus fucking Christ, I am such a –

MIRANDA. What happened?

NICK. He . . . I . . .

Beat.

MIRANDA (*suddenly very curious*). What happened?

Pause.

He looks at her, utterly defeated.

NICK. I . . .

Beat.

Oh fuck. He won't come back now.

MIRANDA. What did you do?

NICK. I . . . was a total . . .

She formulates an idea of what might have happened.

MIRANDA (*with great compassion*). Oh, Nick . . .

76

NICK. I didn't know what to do. And he . . . he . . .

MIRANDA. Yeah . . . ?

NICK. I was . . . I didn't know . . .

Beat.

He won't come back now.

MIRANDA. Yeah. He will.

NICK. No he won't.

MIRANDA. He will. He's just gone to get pizza.

Beat.

He takes this in. He is relieved, almost to tears.

NICK. Oh fuck. Oh fuck oh fuck oh fuck –

She laughs to herself.

What do I do?

Pause.

She approaches him, places one hand on his forehead, the other on the nape of his neck. He cowers.

Stop it, what are you –

He's suddenly sleepy. She struggles to support his weight.

MIRANDA. Careful.

NICK. . . . . What are you . . . ?

MIRANDA. Shh . . .

NICK. It tickles.

She holds him. He is entirely in her power. She rocks him back and forth.

What . . . ?

MIRANDA. Close your eyes.

NICK. No.

MIRANDA. Then I'll close mine.

She does.

Now what are you going to do when he comes back through that door?

NICK. What am I going to do?

MIRANDA. That's what I'm asking.

NICK. Well . . . I . . .

MIRANDA. Not good enough.

NICK. How am I supposed to know what to do?

Beat.

She hugs him hard.

MIRANDA. I have to go.

NICK. No!

MIRANDA. You're on your own, kid.

She gets up to leave.

NICK. Miranda!

MIRANDA. You know I'd do anything for you, don't you?

He looks to her, astonished.

Beat.

NICK (*deflecting*). You wouldn't drink out of that cup.

MIRANDA. Yeah, anything except drink your piss.

She hugs him hard.

She gets up to leave.

NICK. Don't go.

MIRANDA. He'll be back soon.

NICK. Don't go.

She looks at him sadly.

Don't.

Pause.

She leans in close and whispers to him.

She stands and surveys the room: the plastic windmills, the pebbles, the water pistols, snorkels, Frisbees and gonks.

MIRANDA. Look at all this shit. I think I did quite well, don't you?

He's asleep.

I'm taking this though.

She picks up the staff.

If you want a job done properly.

She leaves.

Time passes.

Scene Eleven

Dawn has broken. A low, distant thunder.

NICK *is asleep.* WILLIAM *enters wearing a heavy coat and carrying a large holdall.*

WILLIAM (*whispering*). Nick. Nick, you awake?

Slowly NICK *stirs.*

NICK. You're here.

WILLIAM *holds up a key.*

WILLIAM. I ran into your friend. Or she ran into me. She says you owe her a five-course meal and a bottle of Gordon's. What's that about?

NICK *grunts, still not quite awake.*

Pause.

I brought my stuff. I didn't know if . . . Well, I'm here now.

NICK. You're here.

WILLIAM *bounces his bag on his shoulder.*

WILLIAM. This is everything. I've left the rest behind. But this is everything.

He starts to lay down his bag. NICK gets up and quickly takes it from him. As he does so, he embraces him quickly.

WILLIAM *shivers and yawns.*

NICK. Are you tired?

WILLIAM. What? No. Fresh air. Course, I've been up all night, so I'll have to crash soon, or . . .

NICK. Or what?

WILLIAM. I don't know. I'll turn into a pumpkin or something.

WILLIAM *takes off his coat, followed by a series of shirts.*

NICK *looks on, amused.*

NICK. You look dashing.

WILLIAM. Dashing?

NICK. Like a prince.

WILLIAM. Ha!

NICK. A gallant. Stained with grief.

WILLIAM. Stained?

NICK. Or a siren.

Beat.

I didn't think you'd come. I . . .

Beat.

WILLIAM. Yeah. I know.

Pause.

Tell me about Italy.

NICK. I don't want to talk about that.

WILLIAM. I've never been. Are there mountains?

Beat.

Is it hot?

NICK. It was January.

Pause.

WILLIAM *picks up a book and starts reading the back of it.*

NICK *watches him.*

WILLIAM (*without looking up*). Can I stay here? With you?

NICK *smiles to himself.*

Beat.

WILLIAM *holds up the book* – The Sonnets.

Is it good, this one?

NICK. It's alright.

A low rumble of thunder.

Pause.

I don't know what to –

WILLIAM. Tell me something.

NICK. Tell you what?

WILLIAM. Tell me a story.

Beat.

NICK. I don't know any.

WILLIAM *laughs.*

NICK *takes* WILLIAM's *hands, holds them, studies them,
kisses them. He looks into* WILLIAM's *eyes. He can barely
breathe.*

More thunder. A change in air pressure.

Come unto these yellow sands . . . And then take hands; curt-
sied when you have, and kissed the wild waves whist; foot it
featly here and there, and sweet sprites bear the burden.

Beat.

WILLIAM. And then what?

NICK. And then . . .

He looks at WILLIAM *long and hard.*

WILLIAM *leans in and kisses him, places a hand on his chest.*

WILLIAM. Here?

NICK *places his hand over* WILLIAM*'s hand.*

NICK. Here.

Beat.

Yes, here.

WILLIAM. Yes.

NICK. Yes?

WILLIAM. Yes.

The storm breaks.

They cling to one another.

Appendix of Extracts

I have lost friends, some by death . . . others through sheer
inability to cross the street. I am not so gifted as at one time
seemed likely. Certain things lie beyond my scope. I shall never
understand the harder problems of philosophy.

*

The sun had not yet risen. The sea was indistinguishable from the
sky, except that the sea was slightly creased as if a cloth had
wrinkles in it. Gradually as the sky whitened a dark line lay on
the horizon dividing the sea from the sky and the grey cloth
became barred with thick strokes moving, one after another,
beneath the surface, following each other, pursuing each other,
perpetually.

from The Waves *by Virginia Woolf*

A thing of beauty is a joy forever: its loveliness increases; it will
never pass into nothingness, but will still keep a bower quiet for
us, and a sleep full of sweet dreams . . .

from 'Endymion' by John Keats

Once a man indulges himself in murder, very soon he comes to
think little of robbing; and from robbing he comes next to
drinking and Sabbath-breaking, and from that to incivility and
procrastination.

from On Murder *by Thomas De Quincey*

O Captain! My Captain!

by Walt Whitman

How a ship having passed the line was driven by storms.

*

Water, water, everywhere,
And all the boards did shrink.

*

The water like a witch's oils,
Burnt green and blue and white.

*

And some in dreams assured were
Of the spirit that plagued us so.
Nine fathom deep had he followed us,
From the land of mist and snow.

*

And every tongue, through utter drought,
Was withered at the root;
We could not speak, no more than if
We had been choked with soot.

*

Ah! Well a-day! What evil looks
Had I from old and young!
Instead of the cross, the Albatross
About my neck was hung.

from 'The Rime of the Ancient Mariner'
by Samuel Taylor Coleridge

Additional dialogue from The Tempest, King John *and* Hamlet.

A Nick Hern Book

How To Curse first published in Great Britain as a paperback original in 2007 by Nick Hern Books Limited, 14 Larden Road, London W3 7ST, in association with The Bush Theatre, London

How To Curse copyright © 2007 Ian McHugh

Ian McHugh has asserted his right to be identified as the author of this work

Quotations from *The Waves* by Virginia Woolf by permission of the Society of Authors, as the literary representative of the estate of Virginia Woolf

Cover image: Stem Design
Cover design: Ned Hoste, 2H

Typeset by Nick Hern Books, London
Printed and bound in Great Britain by Biddles, King's Lynn

A CIP catalogue record for this book is available from the British Library

ISBN 978 1 85459 577 5